W9-CBS-749

LEARNING CENTER
Willow Grove School
777 Checker Drive
Buffalo Grove, IL 60089

THE AWFUL AARDVARKS
GO TO SCHOOL

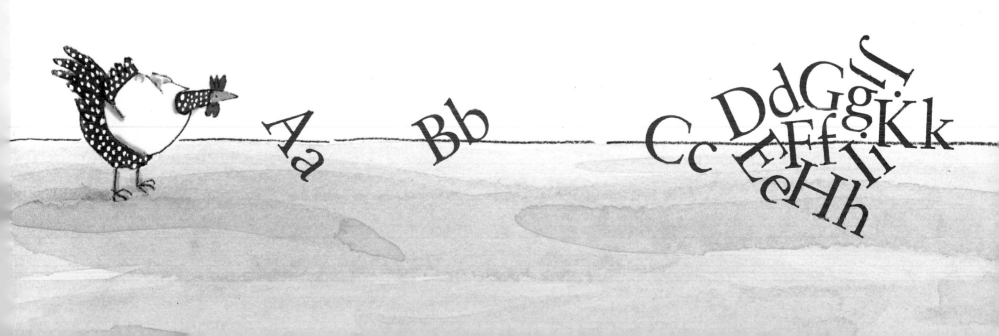

Aa   Bb   Cc DdGg Jj
Ee Ff Kk
Hh Ii

THE AWFUL AARDVARKS
GO TO SCHOOL

LEARNING CENTER
Willow Grove School
777 Checker Drive
Buffalo Grove, IL 60089

BY REEVE LINDBERGH
ILLUSTRATED BY TRACEY CAMPBELL PEARSON

VIKING

LEARNING CENTER
Willow Grove School
777 Checker Drive
Buffalo Grove, IL 60089

VIKING
Published by the Penguin Group
Penguin Putnam Inc., 375 Hudson Street, New York, New York 10014, U.S.A.
Penguin Books Ltd, 27 Wrights Lane, London W8 5TZ, England
Penguin Books Australia Ltd, Ringwood, Victoria, Australia
Penguin Books Canada Ltd, 10 Alcorn Avenue, Toronto, Ontario, Canada M4V 3B2
Penguin Books (N.Z.) Ltd, 182–190 Wairau Road, Auckland 10, New Zealand

Penguin Books Ltd, Registered Offices: Harmondsworth, Middlesex, England

First published in 1997 by Viking, a member of Penguin Putnam Inc.

1 3 5 7 9 10 8 6 4 2

Text copyright © Reeve Lindbergh, 1997
Illustrations copyright © Tracey Campbell Pearson, 1997
All rights reserved

LIBRARY OF CONGRESS CATALOGING-IN-PUBLICATION DATA
Lindbergh, Reeve.
The awful aardvarks go to school / by Reeve Lindbergh ;
illustrated by Tracey Campbell Pearson.   p.   cm.
Summary : An alphabetical listing of the acts of destruction committed by mischievous
aardvarks on their animal classmates during a visit to school.
ISBN 0-670-85920-6
[1. Aardvark—Fiction. 2. Animals—Fiction. 3. Schools—Fiction.
4. Alphabet. 5. Stories in rhyme.] I. Pearson, Tracey Campbell, ill. II. Title.
PZ8.3.L64115Aw 1997 [E]—dc21 97-8820 CIP AC

Printed in U.S.A.
Set in OptiFranz Fifty-Seven

Without limiting the rights under copyright reserved above, no part of this publication may be reproduced, stored in or introduced into a
retrieval system, or transmitted, in any form or by any means (electronic, mechanical, photocopying, recording or otherwise), without the prior
written permission of both the copyright owner and the above publisher of this book.

For Jill Louisa, with love,
and for the Clayton family—thanks awfully!
R. L.

For Emily, Sarah, Mitchell, Henry, and Jackie.
T. C. P.

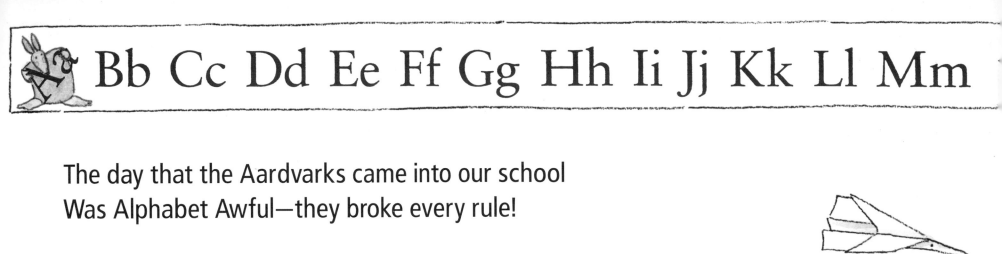

The day that the Aardvarks came into our school
Was Alphabet Awful—they broke every rule!

They Angered the Anteater, Ate All the Ants,
And Bullied the Bunny (they pulled down his pants).

They Chased all our Chickens, they Chewed on a Chair,
Drew Dreadful Drawings, and Danced with the bear.

Nn Oo Pp Qq Rr Ss Tt Uu Vv Ww Xx Yy Zz

Aa B b Cc D d Ee Ff Gg Hh Ii Jj Kk Ll Mm

Even the Elephant wants to forget
That terrible day—but she can't forget yet.

Aa B b Cc D dEe FfGg Hh Ii Jj Kk Ll Mm

Such Fighting! Such Fooling! The class was agog
When those Aardvarks Flicked Fleas at our Friend Freddie Frog.

They Gobbled Green Gum. They were Gross, they were Greedy.
They Hassled our Hamsters—Hank, Hamlet, and Tweedy.

Ignoring Instructions, they clogged up the sink,
Immersed all the Inchworms, and dipped them in Ink.

They Jumped off the Jungle gym, smirking big smirks.
The next thing we knew they were Kissing, the jerks!

The Llama's new Lunchbox they Launched like a rocket,
Which Made the Mice hide in Mike Monkey's pocket.

They nabbed Nellie Newt's Noodle Necklace and tossed it.
(The Ostrich just grabbed it, before Nellie lost it.)

Polly Penguin protested, "Poor Nellie! She's scared."
The Quail Quints Quit Quarrelling Quickly and stared.

But the Aardvarks Ran Riot! They Raced down the halls,
They Showed off, they Shoved Sheep, they Tossed Turtles like balls!

Understand if you will, it was Utterly awful,
Those Vandals were Vicious, and Very unlawful.

When we said, "You're eXpelled!"
Yes, they Yammered and Yelled,

And they wept, "Boo hoo hoo!
Oh poor me! Oh, poor you!"

Aa B b Cc D dEe F Gg H h Ii Jj K k Ll M m

Then they Zoomed to the Zoo—
And *there* what did they do?

I don't even dare to imagine—do you?

LEARNING CENTER
Willow Grove School
777 Checker Drive
Buffalo Grove, IL 60089